marketing

a love story

HOW TO MATTER TO YOUR CUSTOMERS

Bernadette Jiwa

Published in Australia by The Story of Telling Press.

www.thestoryoftelling.com

Portions of this book have appeared previously on
TheStoryofTelling.com blog.

Library of Congress Cataloging-in-Publication Data

Jiwa, Bernadette
Marketing: A Love Story / by Bernadette Jiwa
p. cm.
1. Marketing. 2. Business Development. I. Title.
II. Title: Marketing: A Love Story

ISBN 978-1500619213

Printed in the United States of America

Jacket Design: Reese Spykerman

Book Design: Kelly Exeter

10 9 8 7 6 5 4 3 2 1

First Edition

For Moyez...

*because I can't write a book about love without
dedicating it to you.*

Contents

marketing

a love story

HOW TO MATTER TO YOUR CUSTOMERS

Introduction

'You've got to find what you love. And that is as true for your work as it is for your lovers. Your work is going to fill a large part of your life, and the only way to be truly satisfied is to do what you believe is great work.'
—STEVE JOBS, STANFORD COMMENCEMENT ADDRESS

WHAT'S LOVE GOT TO DO WITH IT?

In the '80s, long before the Internet changed how we shop and before bar codes and scanners came into widespread use, when stores priced things with pricing guns and sticky labels, in pounds and pence with a capital P, my first 'official' job was as a part-time bean counter for a large supermarket chain. Beans were actually a good gig—a doddle compared to a day spent in cold storage counting fish fingers. Every Saturday before the store opened, I would join the other uniformed Stock Control Assistants to receive my clipboard, pencil and instructions from the Stock Controller, whose job it was to make sure that there were enough tins and packets of everything for the customers who would come through the doors the following week.

While I was climbing over pallets of tin cans in the warehouse, customers were taking documented cans—those that had been counted and included in this week's data—off the shelves outside and buying them. As you can imagine, inventory tracking wasn't an exact science, but the company invested a lot of resources in making sure that the job was done.

Because I was part of the stock control team, it wasn't my job to look after customers. If an elderly man approached me to ask if I could tell him where to find the vinegar or could reach a bottle of ketchup from a high shelf while I was counting the last remaining tins of beans in the store, I was supposed to get someone from that department to help him. Usually that person was a shelf filler or a relief checkout operator who also seemed to have a more important role to fulfil.

It struck me as odd that we took so much care to make sure we had enough stock for customers to buy, but we put so few resources into making them feel like we cared or that they mattered once they were actually in the store. We had a team of people to make sure that shelves were full, another team (the marketing department) to make sure that customers came through the door and yet another to get them checked out with maximum efficiency and minimum humanity.

We were heavily invested in the rinse-and-repeat process of getting customers in, selling what was in stock and getting them back out again with the least amount of fuss. We had systems and processes, we provided coupons and discounts, and yet we lost sight of what could have made us really matter to those customers.

I know it seems strange to see the words 'marketing' and 'love' juxtaposed in the same sentence. Marketing is usually billed as that icky thing you have to do to sell more tins of beans, to get attention for your work, your business or your cause, and the only reason to care about it is because it's how you survive. Marketing is supposed to be what you do after you've done the work to create awareness, attract customers, shift more stuff and beat the competition. But what if we thought about the work as marketing, and marketing as the work—as part of a symbiotic relationship where neither could be separated from the other? What if marketing was intrinsic—not something to hand off, but rather something to bake in?

Traditional marketing makes you feel uncomfortable because you know in your heart that you are interrupting people, just as you have been interrupted when you've been on the receiving end. Years of fending off cold calls about average products, ignoring banner ads for services we don't want and changing channels as soon as the adverts come on have taught us that marketing is annoying and the people who do it are not to be trusted.

The interesting thing, though, is that we are all marketers. As humans, we are hardwired to want people to agree with our worldview and belong to our groups. We have had to find ways over the centuries to make people understand us, and although we may not view persuasion in the non-work settings of our life as marketing ('if you eat your greens, you'll grow up big and strong'), that's what it is.

It isn't the 'what' of marketing that has gotten it a bad rap but how we've done it and the shortcuts we have taken in the past. But it turns out that if we work hard to show people that we care, they care back.

Research conducted into how people are persuaded proves that the way we are treated—and the way that treatment makes us feel—affects our opinions and our behaviour. We give bigger tips (as much as 21% more) to waiters who offer us chocolate at the end of our meal, and we buy more tickets from someone who previously demonstrated empathy towards us. People can't help wanting to give back the kind of behaviour or service that they receive, and if we can find ways to authentically show our customers that they matter to us, then we have a better chance of mattering to them.

All the ideas, technology and domain knowledge in the world are worthless unless we can find ways to communicate why people should care about them. The difference between a good idea and a commercial success is *context*—the understanding about where that idea might fit and be useful in the world.

It took at least forty years for the computer to go from being a series of ideas and advances to being a commercial success. It wasn't until companies like IBM, Apple and Microsoft began to figure out a key principle that the magic happened. What made all the difference was the realisation, as Nicholas Negroponte put it, that computing was not about computers but about living.

One of the biggest challenges an entrepreneur or innovator has is understanding how to make his ideas resonate. We tend to have no shortage of ideas, but we struggle to tell the story of how they are going to be useful in the world and why they will matter to people. Marketing is the way we communicate how our ideas translate to value for people in a marketplace.

So, rather than think of marketing as a necessary evil, what if we adopted a different view of it? What if marketing was less about promotion or coercion and more about reaching out to people and helping them to solve problems? What if marketing was how we found more ways to do better work and to matter to our customers? What if marketing was where we began our journey towards understanding what people need and want? What if it was our vantage point for seeing the world through the eyes of our customers? What if, before making a pencil stroke or writing a single line of code, every entrepreneur and innovator began by seeing the world through a marketer's lens and asking, 'why will someone care about this?' How different would marketing be then?

We have a choice. To either do work we care about or not. To put ourselves into our work. To love what we do and care about the people we do it for. If this thing or idea you're selling really doesn't matter to you, why would you sell it? Your days are too precious to spend them simply marking time until every Friday evening, when your life begins.

A BRAND CALLED TRUST

We've been branding things from cattle to jewellery and even people for thousands of years. We began by burning our mark into things to signal ownership. When technology and infrastructure gave us access to things beyond our villages, branding began to signal a different type of belonging, one that said 'you can trust this because it has my mark on it'.

A brand became a symbol of trust.

When you think about a modern-day brand like Dyson, what words immediately spring to mind? Innovative, reliable, trusted, cutting-edge, best, leader and so on. Even if you don't own a Dyson product or know the company's back story (from 5,000+ failed prototypes to multibillion-dollar business), you have a sense of the brand. The Dyson brand is more than just a label or an identifier of the products the company makes. It's an emotional anchor to those products, and while a label can be assigned or attached, an emotional anchor is earned.

A great brand is not a mark burned into a product—it's something we want to belong to.

And so it goes for your brand, too.

When we ask people to buy our stuff or to buy into our ideas, we are asking them to put us or our thing before some other option. We are hoping for their loyalty and good will. We are asking them to believe in and belong to, not just to buy.

Don't they deserve the very best of us in return?

HOW THIS BOOK IS ORGANISED

This book is a series of edited popular posts from my blog. Each article is like a tiny love letter to someone who wants to make an impact in the world through her work. It doesn't matter whether you are the CEO of a giant corporation like Microsoft or the lone entrepreneur trying to create a PowerPoint pitch from your laptop while you drink a single cup of coffee in the local café; I wrote this for you.

If you're the sort of person who thinks, 'why would I buy this book when I can read it for free on a blog?' then head over to my blog at TheStoryofTelling.com, where you can read many of these articles in their original versions. But if you do a lot of your business reading online these days and you bookmark the best stuff to come back to and never do, this book is for you.

The ideas are all intertwined, so you'll find some overlap, but the posts are loosely grouped into three main categories:

> **Strategy** — What you do to meet your goal (the long-term plan).
>
> **Context** — Where your goal, product, or service can be useful in the world (the hole it fills in the market or in people's lives, or what it does for them).
>
> **Story** — How you communicate why all of that will matter to customers (the narrative that conveys who you are and what you care about, as well as what customers tell themselves and others about you).

There's something magical about opening a book, either digital or physical, that makes the ideas inside more powerful. Every time I read the passages that people have highlighted from Kindle books on Amazon.com, it feels like a small miracle—because it is. It's not just that you can see your ideas out in the world; it's that you can also see how people have interacted with them and what resonated. Ideas in isolation are worthless; if they have no impact, then they didn't matter. Creation, innovation and entrepreneurship are not just about putting stuff out into the world—art and business alike are about doing things that make a difference. I hope one of the ideas in this book sparks a small miracle for you on your journey to doing that.

Strategy

LIFE AFTER LAUNCH DAY: INTRODUCING THE ONE-PAGE MARKETING PLAN

It's not hard to remember the lead-up to the birth of your first child. Forty weeks of sheer focus on everything from what cheese to eat (or not to eat) to a birth plan that reads like a military operation. I always found it odd that there was a ten-point plan for every eventuality during the twenty hours of labour, and yet we had no plan for how to navigate the next twenty years after that.

Giving birth to ideas is equally seductive. Thoughts about what it will feel like to see your idea (innovation, product, service, book, video, design) in the world are what drives you to push through when the going gets tough. Often, though, that vision begins and ends with launch day, with most of your energy being focused on giving birth to the project.

Day one is easy to imagine—but what's the plan for day two?

On the next page is a roadmap to help you start thinking about life after launch day. This is simply a template of touch points; it doesn't become a plan until you begin to find answers to questions about what the future might look like. Which must be easier to predict than the first twenty years of a child's life.

THE ONE-PAGE MARKETING PLAN

WHY
Your purpose.

WHO
Your ideal customer.

DIFFERENCE
How and why you are better.

PRICE & POSITIONING
The story you want customers to believe about the value you create.

DISTRIBUTION
How you reach people and get your products into their hands.

PLATFORM
Where you tell your story.

PROMOTION STRATEGY
How you tell your story.

CONVERSION STRATEGY
How you deepen relationships with prospective customers.

GROWTH STRATEGY
The plan for attracting more customers.

REFERRAL STRATEGY
The story you give people to tell.

STRATEGY FOR INCREASING TRANSACTION VALUE
How you delight customers.

RETENTION STRATEGY
How you keep customers coming back.

HOW TO WRITE A MISSION STATEMENT—AND TWENTY GREAT MISSION STATEMENTS TO INSPIRE YOU

By definition a mission statement is the official line on the aims and objectives of your organisation. Academic papers have been written about how mission statements must be cogent (possibly one of the ugliest words in the history of the English language in my opinion).

Your mission statement should describe your key market and your contribution. It should explain why your product or service is unique, setting out reasons why a prospective client would, or *should,* choose you. Having a business idea is the easy part; conveying why it should matter to people and why they should pay for it is not as easy as we like to believe. No wonder most businesses find writing a mission statement hard.

If you're stuck, you can try using the handy mission statement generator at http://cmorse.org/missiongen/ to come up with a mission statement like this one:

> 'We will work concertedly to efficiently monetize best practice methods of empowerment to stay pertinent in tomorrow's world.'

Or try this on for size:

> 'We are committed to globally engineer virtual sources while continuing to quickly leverage web 2.0 services.'

Don't laugh! I'm sure you've read many a meaningless mission statement similar to these ones.

You don't need to tie yourself up in knots or overcomplicate things, though. Your mission statement doesn't need to be long and complex; it's simply a promise—your statement of intention. It needs to clarify the answers to the following two questions: What do you do? What happens because you exist?

As you can see from the examples of mission statements below, a single sentence is often enough to say what you need to say.

Warby Parker
To create boutique-quality, classically crafted eyewear at a revolutionary price point.

TED.com
Spread ideas.

Instagram
To capture and share the world's moments.

Patagonia
Build the best product, cause no unnecessary harm, use business to inspire and implement solutions to the environmental crisis.

Twitter
Instantly connect people everywhere to what's most important to them.

Uber
Evolving the way the world moves.

Adobe
Move the web forward and give web designers and developers the best tools and services in the world.

Google

Organize the world's information and make it universally accessible and useful.

GoPro

To help people capture and share their lives' most meaningful experiences with others—to celebrate them together.

Starbucks

Inspire and nurture the human spirit—one person, one cup and one neighbourhood at a time.

Nest

To keep people comfortable in their homes while helping them save energy.

Amazon

To be Earth's most customer-centric company.

Nike

To bring inspiration and innovation to every athlete in the world.

Airbnb

To build a community-driven hospitality company.

Innocent Juices

We're here to make it easy for people to do themselves some good (whilst making it taste nice too).

Lego

Inspire and develop the builders of tomorrow.

Facebook

To make the world more open and connected.

Jamie Oliver

Help as many people as possible eat better food and live a better life.

Virgin Atlantic

To embrace the human spirit and let it fly.

Ocado

To establish the first new supermarket in a generation.

After you write your mission statement, it shouldn't live in a dusty A4 file or be buried on a long-forgotten, never-updated page on your website. And it shouldn't just be something you say. It should be something you live every day, on purpose.

What are you doing right now, today? Why does your business exist? Why does it matter?

Are you actually on a mission, or are you just saying that you are?

THE NUMBER-ONE WAY TO CREATE VALUE IN ANY MARKETPLACE

In an era when we can push a button on our phones to summon a driver, why is shopping for a television still a nightmare? I doubt that there is a single person in the history of the universe who has enjoyed shopping for a TV.

First you wander through row upon row of yellow-stickered, feature-described sameness. Then just when you're semi-sure that the third TV from the end has the best picture quality, the salesperson arrives with some facts that confuse you.

When we design our stores and our businesses to confuse people, we probably do just that. But intentionally making people feel helpless is the world's worst marketing strategy.

When was the last time you stood in your customers' shoes?

Have you taken a tour of your own website recently? Tried to open your packaging? Called your customer support number on the weekend? Or walked through your store on a busy Friday?

If you're ever in doubt about how to create value, simply work out how to make your customers feel good. Then do that.

WHOEVER GETS CLOSER TO THEIR CUSTOMERS WINS

Let's consider how the business world has been turned on its head in less than a decade. We need to think about only fourteen brands in order to understand the shift.

Apple vs. Sony

Amazon vs. Borders

Netflix vs. Blockbuster

Airbnb vs. Hilton

Uber vs. any taxi company

Nest vs. Honeywell

Twitter vs. News Corp.

It turns out that there isn't a single downside to getting closer to the people you want to serve.

How are you getting closer to your customers?

HOW TO BE THE BEST IN THE WORLD

LEGO bricks are the best in the world. Competitors have tried to copy them over the years, but nothing comes close to a real LEGO brick. So what's the secret?

To make a product *that* good, you've got to continually obsess about design and production lines and quality control. But what makes LEGO the best in the world is how and where they begin the process. LEGO design doesn't begin with the brick. It begins with the people who will use it.

The LEGO designer doesn't work hard to make the perfect brick or the best brick in the world. She obsesses about how it will feel for five-year-old hands to put two bricks together and then pull them apart. She spends her days understanding how it feels to sit on the floor for hours, making a model that won't fall to pieces when you pick it up. Then she designs the product that makes it possible to experience those feelings.

If you want to be the best in the world, don't start by trying to create the best product or service. Start by figuring out how people want to feel.

WHY WE ADVERTISE

Ad spending is set to increase this year. And yet, some of the smartest and fastest-growing companies on the planet elect to grow their businesses through word-of-mouth by delighting their customers. So, why do we still buy banner ads? Is it because…?

1. Our products and services don't create difference for our customers.

2. We don't spend enough time working out how to fulfil that tiny gap in human desire.

3. We want to raise awareness and stay top of mind.

4. We have the budget.

5. We think it's easier than figuring out how to give people something to talk about.

6. Our competitors do it.

7. We've made something for everyone.

8. We confuse awareness with impact.

9. We're afraid.

10. Or worst of all, we believe that advertising is a shortcut to mattering to customers.

What if, instead of spending all that time and money on deciding how to tell customers who we are, we spent more time and money on being who they want us to be?

SIX STRATEGIES THAT WORK BETTER THAN TRYING TO PREDICT THE FUTURE

1. Focus on doing the best work you can do today.

2. Learn how to see the truth and the opportunity in what's right here, right now.

3. Listen to what's going on around you instead of to the voice in your head.

4. Be grateful for who and what you have in your life at this moment.

5. Decide what matters, then make that happen.

6. Stop worrying about where you'll be this time next year.

HOPE IS NOT A MARKETING STRATEGY

There's a tiny market in Potts Point every Sunday. Each week the stallholders show up and hope. They hope that someone who might be their customer will show up, too. The stallholders sell things that passers-by might want, usually things that they could get somewhere else if they weren't going to buy it on impulse between 8am and 4pm on a lazy Sunday.

The guy selling jewellery made from LEGO has a different strategy. He understands the worldview of the grandmas who come to buy LEGO earrings and necklaces. They don't want to look more stylish or glamorous; they want to feel more connected to their grandchildren. A LEGO-earring-wearing grandma definitely has a cool factor.

The earring maker knows who his customers are and what makes them tick before he sets up his stall, and he creates things just for them. Maybe he also knows that understanding your customers is a better strategy than hoping.

WHAT CUSTOMERS BELIEVE IS YOUR COMPETITIVE ADVANTAGE

Ask any business owner about how his business stands apart from the competition and he'll probably begin with the tangible, the things he can easily explain. 'We offer a more competitive interest rate.' 'Our products have more features.' 'We have better distribution.'

In 2008, Windows was the operating system on 84% of personal computing devices shipped. Today that number is just 28%. It turns out that people aren't just buying software and aren't buying based only on price .

Customers don't often pay for the actual value the product delivers. If they did, $4 cups of coffee wouldn't exist, and people wouldn't buy Macs even though they cost more than PCs. People pay for the intangible value, for what they experience and what they care about.

If you can't finish this sentence, then it might be time for a rethink:

'Our customers love how it feels when they _____ our product or service, because _____.'

Your competitive advantage is what your customers believe, not what you make in the factory.

THE DIMINISHING VALUE OF ACCESS

When a new business opens in your suburb, the first thing they do, with great fanfare, is plaster 'Now Open' signs around the neighbourhood. The 'we've built it, now you'll come' mentality is alive and well in every industry.

My son, along with thousands of other young men and women, is in his first year at university. Most of his classes' lectures are posted online, so he needs a good reason to spend an hour taking two buses and a train to get to those lectures. Like many of his friends, he shows up on the days when his mates will have the same two hours free mid-afternoon, so they can hang out together *after* lectures. Many university students agree that their real education no longer has to happen in a lecture theatre. The information isn't more valuable because it's delivered in person by a guy wearing a blazer in a sandstone building.

Access to both information and stuff was scarce ten years ago. It's not what's valuable now. Just showing up, unlocking the door, and putting on the conference or giving the lecture is no longer good enough. Access is no longer the point.

In a world where everything is a tap or a click away, what matters is not *what* is taught or sold, but *how* it's delivered, and how that made someone feel as she walked out the door.

RETHINKING THE GREAT EMAIL SMASH-AND-GRAB

The world has conditioned us from toddlerhood to understand that 'most' is what matters. Even a two-year-old instinctively knows that having just one more chocolate chip cookie than his sister is a good thing. Life teaches you that the people with the most, win, and so the quest for more begins pretty early on. It becomes part of how you operate, how you value yourself and keep score.

In business, the quest for more has led to marketing without context—a kind of 'great email smash-and-grab' which has left us living in popup hell. The idea is that as long as you get the email address, the view, the like or the retweet, you've won.

The truth is that you never win if you try to make your work resonate with everyone, and 'most' isn't the best measure of a more successful business or a fulfilling life.

I know for a fact that headlines that promise to deliver 'ten steps to marketing success' attract more eyeballs, but if hearts and minds are what you're after, then a more-eyeballs strategy might not be the best one for you.

It's far more important to reach out to the people who care than to take aim at everyone.

SIX WAYS TO BECOME PART OF YOUR CUSTOMER'S STORY

Think about the rituals that punctuate your days. Freshly boiled water poured over scented tea in your favourite mug. Your morning workout. The ten minutes you use to brainstorm ideas in Evernote. Checking email or meeting colleagues at lunchtime. Your ring tone, your playlist. Each ritual adds another layer of meaning to your day, becoming part of your story.

When we have ideas, make things, produce, sell and serve, we often begin by trying to determine how to get our 'thing' into the hands or inboxes of more people. The better strategy might be to determine how to punctuate the right person's day and deliver one moment of anticipated joy or welcome interruption.

How might you do that?

1. **Create compelling content or a great product or service that people enjoy using or coming back for.**
   Instagram, Amazon, Dropbox and Gala Darling.

2. **Change how people feel in the moment.**
   Starbucks, Airbnb wish lists, and copy on packaging like Nudie juices.

3. **Solve a problem (maybe one that people didn't even know they had).**
   Evernote, 7-minute workout apps and Canva.

4. **Give people a story to tell themselves.**
   Macarons, Kickstarter, and yes, even a commodity like milk.

5. **Notice what people already do and find ways that you can either change or become part of those rituals.**
   Warby Parker, Zappos and YouTube.

6. **Make it easy for people to come back.**
   Dollar Shave Club, The Period Store and Netflix.

TEN THINGS A BRAND DOES

A brand…

1. Creates meaning around your product or service.

2. Determines what you sell, where and when.

3. Dictates the price range you can sell at.

4. Influences the kind of customers you can sell to.

5. Changes how people feel about commodities.

6. Sets expectations.

7. Affects the kind of staff you can attract.

8. Demonstrates your values.

9. Shapes business models.

10. Enables loyalty, connection, belonging and love.

HOW TO GET THE WORLD TO BEAT A PATH TO YOUR DOOR

Traditional marketing, in essence, has been about doing something today in the hope that your business will reap the rewards in sales tomorrow. With her eyes firmly fixed on the future, the marketer then asks the question, 'what do I need to do to get us from here to there?'

And yet the best marketing happens in the moment, when the entrepreneur, CEO, waiter, designer or developer takes the time to quietly practice empathy. We are at our very best when we see the world through the eyes of the person we're trying to matter to.

That's easy to write and much harder to do than it sounds.

The key to mattering to your customers is to actually care about them just as much as, if not more than, you do about the success of your business. One of the values of the renowned design firm IDEO is to 'make others successful'—as they say, 'going out of your way to help others succeed is the secret sauce.'

Perhaps the question we should be asking, one we don't ask half often enough, is:

'What can we do to get our customers from here to there?'

If you do that often enough, the world will beat a path to your door.

THINKING ABOUT YOUR ASSETS

Take a blank page. Draw a line down the centre. On one side, list your tangible assets, things like stock, equipment, products and your website.

On the other side, make a list of your intangible assets, stuff like intellectual property, trademarks, brand names, the skills of your team, your customer database, your reputation and the trust you have built over time.

Now, one by one, cross off the things that your competitors can easily replicate or acquire, on both sides of the list.

> **Tangible assets**
> ~~Stock~~
> ~~Website~~
> ~~Equipment~~
> ~~Cash balances~~
> ~~Product lines~~
> ~~Property~~

Intangible assets
~~Brand name~~
~~Logos~~
~~Trademarks~~
~~Patents~~
~~Formulas~~
~~Customer database~~
~~Skills~~
Reputation
Customer loyalty
Trust

What are you left with?

As we build our businesses, we often work hardest on the things that are replaceable, believing that our advantage is in the tangible value we provide and can demonstrate. The cup of coffee brewed, the line of perfect code written. But in a world where there are six cafés on every street and 200,000 programmers for hire on Elance in two clicks of a mouse, we need to think more deeply about what really matters to our customers and clients. People place a premium on the things that you can never hand them over the counter (real or virtual). It turns out that trust is the scarcest resource we have.

If you want to build a truly great business, put your energy into the things that can't be crossed off the list.

THE LIMITATIONS OF KNOWING 'HOW TO'

For years we've been rewarded for knowing the right answer. All of those gummed gold stars, licked and stuck in copybooks next to neatly spaced handwriting, served their purpose. We can't help wanting to know the answer.

Knowing 'how to' is barely an advantage to the twenty-first-century business owner or entrepreneur, because there is no one right answer. There is no one way to get to where you want to go—and that's a *great* thing! If there were a 'how to' guide, then everyone would have the formula and nothing we created would be unique.

Nobody told Jobs and Wozniak how to build a computer company, let alone how to make it one of the most loved brands in the world, and Howard Schultz didn't get the Starbucks magic from a manual.

Nobody can tell you what to stand for, or how your values, wants and needs should intersect with those of your customers and then manifest as a business, an idea or an experience. Figuring out the destination is hard—but recognising it is more valuable than knowing exactly how you're going to get there. Until you do the hard work of understanding the 'why' and the 'who for', every tactical 'how to' has the potential to take you down the wrong track.

The most useful answers are the ones we take time to figure out for ourselves—not the ones that everyone can find in a handbook.

Having your own map is more powerful than having someone else's directions. Once you have that map, you'll always have a way to get from where you are to where you want to go.

THIRTY QUESTIONS EVERY ENTREPRENEUR SHOULD ANSWER

We've become really good at looking for answers. So good, in fact, that we get close to asking a billion questions every day in Google search.

And yet as busy business owners and idea creators, we struggle to find time to ask really important questions of ourselves. Here, then, are questions worth taking the time to answer.

1. Why are we doing this?

2. Why are we the people to do it?

3. Why is now the time to start?

4. What will happen because this idea exists?

5. How will this change how people feel about x?

6. Who is it for?

7. Why will they care?

8. What do the people we hope to serve want?

9. What do they believe?

10. How do they feel about the problem we solve?

11. What do they do—where, when, why and with whom?

12. What will customers say to their friends to recommend this product or service?

13. How can we make customers feel good because they recommend the product or service?

14. What are we really selling beyond the utility of the product or service?

15. How can we add more value?

16. What happens because our business or project exists?

17. How will people find us?

18. Where are they already looking, or not looking?

19. What's our greatest strength?

20. What weakness might get in the way if we don't address it?

21. What does success look like today, this year, next year and five years from now?

22. What do we value?

23. What do we want to change?

24. What promises do we want to make and keep?

25. What matters most right now?

26. What's going to matter more three, six or eighteen months from now?

27. What's our difference?

28. What do we need to do today, to make sure that we can keep doing the things we want to do tomorrow?

29. If we could do anything today, would this be it?

30. If not this, then what?

When you know what you want, where you're headed and why, almost nothing can stop you.

GREAT CONTENT MARKETING DOESN'T FEEL LIKE MARKETING

> *'You're more likely to summit Mount Everest than you are to click on a banner ad.'*
> —JONATHAN PERELMAN, VP, BUZZFEED

Getting the word out about your products and services can feel a bit like an Everest expedition.

You and I know that traditional advertising doesn't work anymore. We've known from as far back as 2005 that the return on investment from advertising could be as little as 4%. Then along came a new marketing 'secret sauce', a way to attract customers and gain their loyalty—all we had to do was create content.

It's tempting to think that we can use content in the way that we once used traditional advertising to attract the most people. The best content, though, goes beyond simply being advertorial and appealing to everyone. Why do you return to your favourite blogs? What makes you share the content you choose to share?

The secrets of great content marketing

1. Great content changes how people feel by being either useful, entertaining or inspiring.

Think about how you want your readers to feel as they read the last line of your article. What do you want them to do next? That doesn't mean getting them to click on a 'BUY NOW' link every time.

2. Your products and services help clients and customers to be better versions of themselves every day, so your content should be designed to do that, too.

Building trust in and connection to you and your brand over time, rather than promotion, is the point. Great content doesn't feel like marketing—it feels like a gift.

3. Content marketing, like all your marketing, isn't something separate from your work but is an extension of it.

Authentically bake it into your business; don't just slap it on as an afterthought to fill white space and create noise. Use content to help people to understand more about who you are and what your business stands for.

4. Don't see your content as a big old sales funnel.

Treat it more like a flame, a campfire that people want to come back to. Intention is everything. People can sense yours; they know when you're in it for the right reasons.

5. Practice patience.

The reason we got into this fix was that we tried to take the shortcut to mattering to our customers. An advert that could blast hundreds of thousands of people felt like a bargain. It turns out, though, that it was a Trojan horse that destroyed our relationships with our customers. The people, brands and businesses that have the traction you're craving have been creating content and providing value to their audiences for years. There's nothing to stop you from doing that, too.

Plant your flag. Bring people with you.

DON'T MAKE ME CLICK, MAKE ME CARE

There's no denying it—calls to action are important and increasingly so in a world of infinite choices. We have less and less time to give people a reason to choose us.

Calls to action matter, not just because we want people to do certain things when they visit our website but because people like to understand what they need to do next. Your readers and your customers appreciate it when you make life easy for them. But we all know how annoying it feels to experience the 'hard sell' even when the salesperson isn't in the room with us. Popups that appear before we read a single word and BUY-NOW-button mania only serve to make us do the opposite of what was intended.

So how on earth do you find a balance? How do you make people click?

You need to start by asking a better question. Your website shouldn't be optimised just to make people click what you want them to click. Your website needs to make people feel like they belong. When they do, they want to return and to become members, customers and advocates.

Helping people to feel like they belong is a better long-term strategy than finding ways to make them click and pay.

Don't make people click. Find ways to make people care.

DO YOU HAVE A HUMAN BUSINESS STRATEGY?

When I was a little girl, buying new shoes was always an event. We went to a local shoe shop, the one that advertised the credentials of their 'specially trained fitters'. We patiently waited our turn for the magic that was about to happen. This usually involved a matronly woman and what was essentially a metal ruler in the crude shape of a shoe. The green plastic strap that she threaded around your instep to measure the width of your foot was important, of course. This was science and not art, after all.

And yet when we think about the job of the sales assistant back then, we understand that everything she did was an art. The art of understanding her customers enough to know that a ritual was required. The art of building trust. The art of reassuring a man—who, as one of eleven children, had walked out of school for the last time at the age of thirteen without shoes on his feet—that spending half a week's wages on an impossibly small amount of black patent leather was the right thing to do if you wanted to give your little girl the world.

It felt good to be able to sit and wait patiently for the small stack of green boxes to appear from behind the curtain, to have the assistant carefully buckle the shoes up and then to 'take a little walk up and down' to make sure that they weren't slipping.

We bought more than something to cover small feet with those worn green notes.

While the whole world has turned on its head in the forty years between then and now, some things haven't changed at all and it's those things that as business owners we really need to pay attention to. Experts, technologists and futurists will tell you that you need to be agile, to be ready to move with the times and embrace a multi-screen world that is changing right before your eyes.

The platforms and tactics we use to reach our customers in a digital world keep changing, but the strategy for touching human beings who make decisions with their hearts and not their heads remains the same.

THREE ESSENTIAL MARKETING QUESTIONS

As marketers, we invest a great deal of time and money in figuring out how to tell the story of our products. But if we can agree that marketing is giving people something to talk about, why aren't we using resources in equal measure to do that?

What if we began with a new set of questions?

1. Who *exactly* do we want talking about our product or service?

2. What do we want them to say?

3. How will we make sure it happens?

If this sounds simple and obvious, the fourth question is, why haven't we done it?

THINKING ABOUT MARKETING AS A STRATEGY FOR GROWTH, NOT JUST SALES

Mostly we market to sell more.

The restaurant owner who tells his staff to remember to push drinks and bottled water is marketing for increased sales today.

The alternative is to be the marketer who bakes growth into his business by delighting customers, giving them a story they want to tell (and a way to share it).

The modern marketers at technology startups call this technique 'growth hacking'. Growth hackers optimise their businesses to acquire new customers by first delighting one customer and then making it easy for that customer to share the story with friends. They win by delivering on a promise, by connecting customers and having a plan not just to sell more to each customer today but to give every person more to talk about and an easy way to do that.

Last year, hotels in New York lost out on a million booked nights because of Airbnb. The strategy of most hotels has been to maximise revenue from each captive guest, while Airbnb's has been to facilitate a real travel experience, one guest and one host at a time.

It turns out that growth hacking is really the practice of creating and leveraging word-of-mouth with intention, and it's not confined to technology businesses. When we market for long-term growth and not just sales, we adopt a different posture. We're in the business of doing the right thing by every customer over time and we begin each day by asking a different set of questions.

The salesperson asks, 'How much can I sell?'

The gifted modern marketer asks, 'How much difference can I create?'

NO BUSINESS IS IN A MARKET OF ONE (BUT YOU DON'T HAVE TO FOCUS ON THE COMPETITION)

When dance partners compete, they know that the other couples are there on the dance floor with them, but they never focus on what the competition is doing. Instead they relentlessly hone each move and perform it for the audience as if it were their only chance to dance the dance. They don't allow the fact that they are competing to stop them from dancing.

It's our competition's job to compete and yet we're often surprised when they do. We complain when ideas are stolen or replicated. We spend at least as much time looking over our shoulder at the competition as we do on practicing our steps in readiness for the performance.

What would the world look like if you focused on doing the work as if today were the last time you would get to do it?

You can allow the noise from the competition to fade into the background. You can choose to act as if you were the market of one for the people you want to serve.

THE QUESTION YOUR CUSTOMERS ARE REALLY ASKING

And the one you must spend a great deal of your time answering:

Why should I care?

- Why should I care about your new app?
- Why should I care that your innovation pioneers the latest technology?
- Why should I care about your fundraising campaign and not that other organisation's?
- Why should I care about the time you've invested in elegant design?
- Why should I care that you showed up today to play that tune?

In a world of finite time and infinite choices, it's easier than ever before to rationalise walking past. The only way to matter is to first determine what matters. You need to give people a reason to stop and listen to your song.

HOW TO HIT YOUR TARGET

When an archer aims, she doesn't keep her eye on the target. She knows the target is there, but she sees it vaguely or sometimes not at all. The point of aim is always closer than the target.

Hitting the target is determined by how she aims, not by the fact that she's shooting for it.

So much of our business practice is focused on some future outcome—a key performance indicator, a better bottom line, another successful round of funding, more subscribers, an uptick in the number of orders—and the moment that we hit the target. But if we hit our targets, it's not because we continually focus on them; we know the target is there, but the target is not the focus. The focus is on how we aim—on doing the right thing today and then building on that by doing it over and over again.

Your target is not some distant outcome or a metric of tomorrow; your target is how you're aiming right now.

WHAT'S MORE IMPORTANT THAN BUILDING AWARENESS?

Ask any business owner what his most pressing problem is and 'building awareness' is sure to be on the list. Maybe it's on your list, too? In a world where it's harder to get attention, gaining mind share is a priority for everyone.

We think that if we can just get a few more people to know about us, we'll be all set.

I often tell the story of the two side-by-side cafés in our neighbourhood.

On days when there is a line of twenty people waiting for either a table or a takeaway coffee at one café, the other is virtually empty. We all know the empty café is there—we can't miss it—and yet nothing changes. It's not that the owners don't care; it's that all of their energy is focused on tactics that get people to notice (and it appears that those tactics aren't working).

Perhaps the bigger questions for those café owners to consider (and maybe us, too), before building awareness with more signs and new menus, is, why will one person care that we're here in the first place? What are we doing that's going to compel that person to tell two friends and then come back tomorrow?

What's more important than building awareness is what you plan to do with it once you've got it, because top of mind is not the same thing at all as close to heart.

ATTENTION IS NOT OUR SCARCEST RESOURCE

If you want to capture someone's attention, you've got about ten seconds to convince him that you are the one. Attention spans are shrinking. People have so many demands, diversions and distractions right there in their pockets every minute of every day that it's getting harder and harder to hold their interest. This is the reason that whole industries still exist to find ways to capture attention. But what if attention isn't actually the scarcest resource?

When a new café opens in your neighbourhood, you'll give it a try, but that initial visit is no guarantee that you'll keep going back. You might buy pizza when they are selling two-for-one on a slow Tuesday night, but that doesn't mean that the store owner has done enough to see you there on a Friday. Headlines designed to bring as many strangers to your blog as possible this week might not make for a community of evangelists in the long run.

There's something that's harder to cultivate than attention. Something that there is no formula for getting. Something that can't be captured, but has to be nurtured instead. That something is a feeling of connection and belonging.

When we build our businesses around a single shot at getting someone's attention for a short-term gain today, we're wasting an opportunity to build a business that endures. The smart brands of the new millennium have thrived on this notion of building for belonging. The Apples, Starbuckses and Airbnbs of the world understand that they are playing a long game. They understand that the conversation isn't over after the first interaction, and they find ways to bake the chances of another connection into their company's infrastructure and DNA.

'That's all very well for big corporations', you might say; 'we just don't have the resources to do that kind of thing and time is not on our side. We need eyeballs and bums on seats today!'

I know, I know—I really do—but it's more important to create deeper connections with the right people to make your business sustainable.

Once when I was visiting a new city, I did a scout-around for a place that sold good coffee—it's usually the spot that isn't on the main street, the place where you see the locals hanging out. I took a chance, had a great experience and was on my way. The next day, I thought, 'why mess with success?' and headed back to the same café. The guy who took my order the day before asked if I'd like a … and he rattled off my non-standard coffee order from the day before. Boom, a shot of oxytocin and a feeling of instant connection and belonging. I don't know how this guy ended up being 'that guy who remembers people by their coffee orders', but I bet his boss is glad that he did.

You've got to find a way to be 'that guy' for the people you want to serve. The one who is patient enough to take the time to make them feel like they belong. If you're in this for the long haul, you don't need the shortcuts that you're hoping will magically deliver more people to your door today.

ATTENTION IS A TWO-WAY STREET

Do you know what's really ironic? Businesses spend thousands of dollars, plus manpower, head space and creative energy, trying to get the attention of potential customers, and when they get it, they waste it. The question for all of us (not just in business but also in life) is, how can we expect what we're not prepared to give?

You can test out this theory anywhere you do business today, in the café, grocery store, cinema and on and on. Everywhere you go, people will be multitasking. Having their morning tea break while they fill orders at their desks. Answering the phone while they delete email. Serving a customer while they talk to their colleague at the next checkout.

We work hard to get people over the line; then we don't even bother to give them eye contact. There's no excuse for this. Even if your business is online, you have to find a way to give people virtual eye contact. Zappos built a billion-dollar business on that single difference.

It seems that hardly anyone takes the time to properly pay attention anymore, to do just one thing. *Your customers want to be that one thing.* They want to feel like they matter. If you don't make them feel that way when they walk through the door, what's the point of opening the door in the first place?

All the marketing tactics in the world won't save us from our own indifference.

PICK ONE THING

When you think of Apple, you immediately think about great design. You are reminded that Apple chooses to lead with design even in the moments between the moments that matter to you as a customer. It's hard not to be in awe of a company that cares so much about your experience that they make the packaging feel like a gift.

Patagonia leads with transparency. It's not always easy to tell your customers the truth, but once you make that decision, every subsequent decision becomes easier.

Zappos chooses to lead with service. This choice underpins everything they do, from whom they hire to how they treat their staff and customers.

Peter and Anca of Happy Flame lead with love. They don't make the most candles, and they hug their customers every day.

The secret of all great companies (big and small) is that they choose. They understand how they create value and they do it on purpose, with intention.

What are you choosing to lead with?

THE BUSINESS CASE FOR CREATING GREAT CUSTOMER EXPERIENCES

According to a report published by Genesys in 2009, the total cost of poor customer service in the 16 countries surveyed was USD$338.5 billion. The cost of poor customer service in the U.S. alone was $83 billion.

The same global survey found that 70% of our customers leave, never to return, because they were not made to feel like they mattered. Of course they don't just vanish into the ether; they go to the competition. So poor service not only damages our bottom line, but also widens the gap between us and our competitors.

We spend hundreds of billions of dollars every year trying to get people to notice us, and once we get them through the door, we don't take care of them. In a world with so many choices, it's no longer good enough to show up and open the door. Smart marketers understand that it's how the door is opened—and what happens after the door is opened—that matters.

Context

DITCH THE BUSINESS PLAN AND WRITE A LETTER TO YOUR FUTURE CUSTOMER

This might sound like a pointless and obvious exercise that's easy to do, so why would anyone bother? I guarantee you that if more of the forgettable businesses you've visited and never been back to had written this letter (or their own version of it), they'd be one step closer to remarkable.

Time to ditch the business plan for a second and begin.

Dear _____,

It was great to hear from you today. I remember the day I saw you struggling to _____; a hundred light bulbs went off when I realised at that moment that I could help you to _____.

I know that you want to do/create/be/feel/have _____ and I understand the challenges you face, like _____ and _____, because over the past five years I've been working on/ helped _____ to overcome similar problems. Understanding your experience is the reason I created _____.

Here's how it works.

Once you begin/finish/buy/use _____, you will be able to _____. And that's the reason I can't wait to jump out of bed and get to work every morning.

You can try/start/buy it now [hyperlink]. If you have any questions, you can contact me any time at getitnow@whatyouvebeenwaitingfor butdidntknow.com

Best wishes,
Alex
CEO, whatyouvebeenwatingforbutdidntknow.com

HOW APPLE SUCCEEDED WHILE OTHERS FAILED

When Apple designed their first store, they made sure that over half of it was dedicated to what they called 'solutions'. The store wasn't stacked ceiling to floor with inventory; instead, it was a wall-to-wall space of discovery.

While most retailers were showing people what they had in stock, Apple was showing people what their products could help them become. The Apple strategy was built around Steve Jobs' understanding that 'people don't just want to buy personal computers anymore, they want to know what they can do with them'.

That single insight sums up the key to Apple's success. What Jobs recognised was that increasing sales, growth and market share is a side effect of understanding what people really want.

He didn't give people reasons to choose. He gave them reasons to crave, to covet and to belong.

How could you do that for your customers?

REDEFINING WHAT IT MEANS TO GO VIRAL

Your idea is not a virus and here's why: A virus doesn't care who it infects. Everyone is a target.

A virus's only reason to be a virus is to survive. But you actually care about the people who use your products, read your book, or sign up for your service. You are not in the business of survival; you want to create a difference for the people you serve.

How to 'go viral' with intention

1. Create something that people want.

2. Know whom you want to infect.

3. Have a great reason for wanting to infect them.

4. Matter to one person first. Speak to that person.

5. Change how people feel, before you try to change what they do.

6. Notice what your customers care about most. Do more of that.

7. Work hard to give people something to talk about. Kittens don't count.

8. Consciously bake word-of-mouth into your product or service. Most people skip this step.

9. Make giving people a reason to talk about your products and services part of your culture, not just your marketing.

10. Do it on purpose. Then do it over and over again.

The businesses that succeed wildly are not just founded on ideas that are shared in a split second; they are grounded in what will matter to their customers for decades.

THE BIGGEST PROBLEM FACING ENTREPRENEURS

…is love. People with great ideas (and average ones, too) are in love with the ideas themselves. Because we're human, we become irrationally seduced by the potential of our own solutions. This infatuation blinds us to what matters most, to the thing that gives an idea the best chance to fly.

Being in love with the idea is what made the Segway falter. It's also what made the BlackBerry fall into the abyss and made Kodak flounder after decades of domination.

Of course you've got to believe in the product, service, or solution you're creating. But what you need more than a love of your product is love for your customers. You have to care about them to want to make something for them. And you have to understand them to care about them.

Understanding of the customer is why Apple's packaging feels like a gift. It's the reason Instagram became unstoppable and how Lululemon amassed a cult following.

When you innovate and build your business from a place of empathy and a desire to create difference for your customers, those values bubble up into everything you do.

THE TROUBLE WITH POSITIONING

Do you remember when President Obama came to office the first time 'round and negotiated with the Secret Service to keep his BlackBerry? Presidents Bush and Clinton didn't even use email. In 2004, three years before the launch of the first iPhone, Research in Motion, which created the BlackBerry and pioneered the smartphone, had a market share of 47%. In 2009, RIM was the fastest-growing company in the world. Today its share of the smartphone market is just 2% and the BlackBerry is facing obsolescence.

The company (renamed as BlackBerry Ltd. in 2013) had identified, occupied and dominated a product niche by developing a phone that could email. It was perfectly positioned to stay top of mind for years to come.

I think where they came unstuck was in believing that their job as innovators was to change how people felt about their product, instead of wondering how smartphones might shape culture beyond giving people the ability to check email on the go. In the end, BlackBerry didn't lose out because of Apple and Google; they lost out by failing to understand how their brand would enable connection going forward.

The trouble with positioning is that it doesn't take into account that business is symbiotic, that the relationship between brand and customer really is interdependent. That's because positioning is less about considering what people value and more about telling people what to believe.

It's not enough to be first to market or top of mind. The brands that we care about don't just make innovative products; they shape our culture and make us feel like better versions of ourselves. They take into account what we believe, how we act and who we might want to become. Which is very different from riding the wave of first-mover advantage.

Brands big and small connect people through a culture that's bigger than themselves—through provenance, adventure, sustainability, entrepreneurship, self-expression, conscious consumption, sisterhood and real food, to name a few movements.

So tell me, what beliefs are you connecting your customers to?

THE ELEVEN WHYS OF PRODUCT DEVELOPMENT

In my work with companies, entrepreneurs and businesses of all stripes, here's what I've found: We mostly get stuck not because we don't know the right answer but because we haven't begun to ask the right questions.

Here's a handy list of questions to ask *before* you bring your product, service or idea to market.

1. Why are we making this?

2. Why doesn't this exist already?

3. Why us?

4. Why now?

5. Why do people need this product?

6. Why will people *want* this product?

7. Why will people pay for this?

8. Why will this make people do/feel/be what they want to do/feel/be?

9. Why would people buy from our competitors?

10. Why will people cross the street to buy from us?

11. Why does this idea matter?

The truth is that often we don't know the answers to all of the questions. Sometimes even after we've answered the questions, we've just got to take our best guess and go.

THE UNCOMMON ADVANTAGE

In the '80s, you'd walk into a record shop, and the store owner, along with the record company, would literally tell you what to buy. In every store, there was a wall with a hundred square compartments, labelled, unsurprisingly, TOP 100. You got to choose from what everyone else liked or what DJs were playing that week. The mainstream, the normal.

Telling people what to believe and what to buy worked for a little while, but it's not working so well now. Now it's cool to be the guy who discovered the little band from Texas before the rest of the world knew about them. People don't want to be mainstream or normal. They no longer want a choice of rock or pop, punk or disco, this or that.

People aren't just buying 'different'; they are making choices right out there on the edges, as far out on the precipice as it's possible to go. People want what they want, not what the world tells them they can have.

We have witnessed the end of 'or' and the rise of the uncommon advantage, which leaves untapped markets, unfulfilled needs and unspoken desires ripe for discovery, reinvention and innovation.

The world is waiting for you.

WHAT IF YOU'RE NOT CLOSER, FASTER OR CHEAPER?

There was no size 12 in stock at the local department store, but 'the system' was showing two identical black dresses: one in the City store, the other equally far away. Neither dress was actually there, as it turned out—something that I discovered only by getting in my car and driving to both stores only to come away empty-handed. And as I stood there in the half-empty shopping centre on what should have been a busy Saturday afternoon, I remembered why the department stores are struggling and giving deep discounts.

In a world of infinite choices, where faster and cheaper are two clicks away, and free overnight shipping makes closer increasingly irrelevant, every business must question why people will pay for their services.

The Internet has given plenty of businesses the opportunity to become more relevant to their customers, and it's forced others to question what they are really offering beyond the thing that they wrap up for customers to take home.

The value of everything was always in the meaning and the story we told ourselves about having, owning or doing the thing. The Internet just brought that into sharp focus.

If you can't add value in the moment, then the only opportunity open to you is to add meaning.

What reason are you giving your customers to bypass a hundred (or maybe 100 million) other choices and get in their cars or cross the street to come to you? Opening your doors (even if they are virtual ones) isn't enough anymore.

THE MOST DANGEROUS THING ABOUT YOUR COMPETITION

…is your obsession with them.

Yes, we live in a giant digital goldfish bowl. This makes it possible to get stuck watching and worrying about what our competitors are doing. Almost every move they make—every accolade, acquisition and award—is there for the world to see.

It's far more productive and more profitable to obsess about what your customers are doing and then determine how you could help them to do it with more ease.

While taxi firms worried about the impact of fare hikes associated with rising fuel prices, the founders of the Uber app found ways to add value to the experience of hiring a car instead. Uber created a premium service for customers who were happy to pay extra, and they built a company with an $18 billion valuation in five years—without owning a fleet of cars.

Becoming the competition doesn't always mean using the same old rules to beat others at their own game. Focusing on the tiniest gap in your customers' desires might be a better strategy.

HOW TO SELL A GUITAR—OR ANYTHING

The number-one reason a salesperson fails to close a sale is that she can't effectively communicate the value of the product. Of course it makes sense that if you can't help your customers to understand why they should care, then you're not likely to be able to convince them to buy.

The luthier takes care to choose the perfect piece of wood. She obsesses about the distance between frets and the quality of the strings she uses. But she often forgets to spend time wondering how to tell the customer why any of that should matter to him.

A winning sales strategy doesn't just involve working out how to sell more of what you make. A better plan is to understand what people really value and then to give them exactly that.

Don't sell the guitar. Sell the music.

EMPATHY IS THE KILLER APP

One of the reasons that upstart companies like GoPro have been able to steal a march on their much-better-resourced competitors, like Sony, has been their ability to develop products for their customers by truly understanding who those customers are and what they want.

It's not possible to create products, services or innovations that fly without understanding people first. Google can leverage access to all the money, data and expertise in the world, but the company has struggled to make Google Glass resonate because of lack of empathy, according to one of the product's first evangelists, Robert Scoble, who recently stopped wearing his because of how Glass wearers are perceived. Now, ironically, one of Google's biggest challenges is teaching Glass users how to be empathetic while they are wearing the glasses.

There really is no substitute for standing in your customers' shoes. You can have the best product in the world, but if people don't buy into the story, you've got an uphill struggle on your hands.

WHO DECIDES WHAT WINS

The app developer will spend hundreds of hours writing lines of perfect code in the hope of making his final product the best in the world. The café owner could pull thousands of shots in order to create the perfect cup every time. The entrepreneur might invest months in agonising over design decisions to launch with a more compelling website. The author can labour for years crafting perfect sentences that will surely make his book worthy of a slot on the bestseller list.

And yet—they have less control over what the people who buy their end product believe, feel, think and say than they would like to imagine. When Cadbury 'improved' the shape of their chocolate bars (a decision a behemoth brand would not take or implement lightly), customers pushed back, telling the company in no uncertain terms how much they hated the new shape and how much they wanted the familiar traditional Cadbury bar back.

We might know that our product really is the best in the world, but we're not the ones who get to decide. What we do and what we ask customers to believe are only part of the story. It's humbling to realise that the people we serve, *not* our technologists, publishers, innovators, designers or marketing departments, decide what's worthy and what wins.

HOW TO DISRUPT THE MARKET

Do you remember the days when printed news was so valued that there were two editions of the daily newspaper? People waited at the local shops for evening editions to arrive at 4pm, and paperboys weaved between cars which were stopped at a red light during rush hour, where drivers also waited with exact change to receive the news.

My grownup sons have never bought a newspaper and they never will. They don't wait to receive the news; they make it appear on demand when they want it, on their terms. The double-digit decline in newspaper circulation isn't a surprise and it's certainly not news to anyone anymore.

We might say that the Internet and mobile devices disrupted the print media market. But before innovation can disrupt the market, it must disrupt the moment—that point when a single person feels or perceives something that causes her to change how she acts. Not everyone stopped buying newspapers back in 2007 when Twitter launched. It isn't one sudden seismic shift that creates change, but a billion tiny incremental movements in the moment.

We are often impatient when we want to change how people act (which is why marketing exists, after all). This impatience is the reason health campaigns and other traditional marketing efforts often fail. They try to change everything and everyone all at once. But lasting change doesn't happen that way.

If you want to disrupt your market, look for opportunities to change a single micro-moment, one person at a time.

THE VALUE OF ASKING 'WHAT IF?'

Have you ever been stuck waiting outside your hotel room while it was given the daily once-over? For some guests, housekeeping can feel like more of an intrusion than a service.

On average, it costs a hotel $22 a day to deliver housekeeping services for each room. That figure probably doesn't account for the recruitment of staff and the use of extra towels and linen.

I recently stayed at a Marriott hotel where they were trialling a scheme which offered guests the choice to opt out of housekeeping during their stay in exchange for either restaurant credit or loyalty points. Hardly rocket science, but somehow it felt good to be offered the option and to feel like the hotel had considered my wants and needs as an individual.

Someone had taken time to consider the guest's worldview and asked the question, 'What if some guests value privacy more than a freshly made bed?'

Allowing customers to define what value is for them in this situation makes good business sense, and yet hotels have been using a cookie-cutter guest-services formula forever.

Asking 'what if' feels risky because it means you might have to acknowledge that what you've worked hard to put in place might not be the best solution. But if we don't have the courage to question our assumptions, we're choosing to stagnate by default.

THE ECONOMICS OF ATTENTION

Attention is either earned or paid for. Whether you pay for advertising or not, you still buy your audience's attention every day. You may not pay in dollars and cents, but there is still a cost attached to getting people to notice or engage.

The cost of paid attention in the form of TV ads has been rising faster than inflation since the mid-1990s. The flip side is that the value of that attention is decreasing. More channels, more ads and more choices have translated into less trust, lack of belief and declining motivation to pay attention. On top of that, the way we now consume media, on demand and on our own terms via mobile devices, has changed both our expectations and our behaviour. But apart from making adverts shorter and shifting to different platforms to tell our stories, we're often still guilty of marketing in that 1990s 'Here we are, this is what we've got for you' way. We're still using tactics that worked on a very different customer. They are not working now.

It's not just the economics and the media that have changed—it's your customers. Increasingly, what matters to people is not how you show up, but *why* you show up. The biggest-spending consumers aren't simply shopping for stuff anymore; they are shopping for ways to change how they feel, to express themselves and to find meaning. They no longer want information or even experiences; they expect context—an understanding of what matters to them.

You might not have control over the increasing cost of reaching people or their decreasing attention spans, but you *do* have control over what happens before, after and in the moment that you meet your customers where they are. The future success of your business is less likely to be shaped by all the attention money can buy and much more likely to be shaped by your intention—which is free to choose.

HOW TO BE GREAT

Dr Dre and Jimmy Iovine don't make great headphones because they know the most about headphones. They make great headphones because they understand how music should sound, and more importantly, they know that people want to feel, not just hear, when they listen to it.

> *'The right song at the right time will give you a chill.*
> *Make you pull someone close. Nod your head. Sing in*
> *the mirror. Roll down the car window and crank the*
> *volume to the right.'*
> —Ian Rogers, CEO, Beats Music

Our best ideas and innovations are not born from simply wanting to make them great. We make them great by understanding who they are for and why they should matter.

Understanding what makes people tick and why is far more valuable than we think.

WHAT ARE YOUR CUSTOMERS' TRIGGERS?

We mostly think of buying as an isolated act, something our customers do in the moment. But it's probably more useful to think of buying as a behaviour. A behaviour is an action or reaction which is triggered and conditioned. We look in the fridge at 8pm and notice that we're running low on milk; that's our trigger to jump in the car before the supermarket closes. The light turns green and that's our trigger to go.

Digital entrepreneurs build products and services with apps, games and platforms in ways that trigger certain behaviours. Our use of the digital products and platforms we can't live without is behaviour driven. How long is it before a bored commuter whips out his iPhone while he stands waiting for a bus?

BJ Fogg, who runs the Persuasive Technology Lab at Stanford University, created a simple formula for behaviour change. The Fogg Behaviour Model suggests that for a behaviour to occur, three things need to be in place:

- Trigger—Do this now

- Ability—Can do it

- Motivation—Want to do it

Marketers of physical products have been slower to recognise buying as a behaviour. As marketers, we often think of buying as an exchange that customers can be persuaded into with discounts and special offers. Savvy marketers see buying as a behaviour that they have the power to influence with triggers and not just persuasion. Starbucks built a billion-dollar business by leveraging triggers like the morning commute for able and motivated customers. For people who bought a new pair of eyeglasses only once every two years when their prescription ran out, Warby Parker changed the buying trigger from necessity to fashion-consciousness. Black Milk Clothing releases limited-edition, time-limited product lines. Apple's product launches are triggers of legend.

Triggers lead to actions that can become behaviours. As marketers, we spend a lot of time focusing on our customers' motivation and ability, but as Fogg mentions, we need all three things to be in place to create behaviours, and it's those behaviours that build sustainable businesses. Perhaps we need to start thinking more like great user experience designers?

Don't just focus on the moment your customer pulls out her credit card. Think about how, why and how often she gets to that point and how you might influence those factors in the future.

THE MARKETING SHORTCUT

The fare on sale at the coffee window of our local café changes each morning.

On Monday, homemade protein power balls and muesli bars are strategically laid out to fend off the regret of the weekend's indulgences. On Tuesday, it's fruit-filled muffins, and by Friday, we're splashing out with a chocolate-covered something. All hell breaks loose on Saturday and Sunday when almond croissants, jam-filled doughnuts and bacon and egg rolls are piled high to fuel weekend runs and long coastal walks.

The offerings sell out every single day.

If you care enough to figure out what people are hungry for and why (it's usually not another doughnut or more stuff), then you'll find you do a lot less marketing.

THE PURPOSE OF INNOVATION IN A 'NEEDLESS' ECONOMY

For the most part, in the West, we have everything we need. Roofs over our heads, food in the fridge and a lot more besides. Even in the developing world, where more people have mobile phones than have access to toilets, it seems that sometimes 'wants' trump real needs.

So, if we have everything we need and it's mostly 'good enough', what's the purpose of innovation?

As an innovator or bringer of ideas to the world, you need to make things that add meaning to peoples' lives. Things that change how people feel first, which in turn changes what they do and what they come to expect and embrace.

Just ten years ago, it was impossible to experience something and film it at the same time because we had to hold the camera and use a viewfinder. There was no way to record high-quality video footage of the things we were doing while we were doing them. Entrepreneur and surfer Nick Woodman changed that when he brought a small, wearable video camera (originally intended for surfers) to market. Today, GoPro is the multibillion-dollar company that helps people to record, relive and share their adventures. GoPro cameras are not used simply to document activities—they allow people to become the heroes of their own stories. Even ordinary events, like bike rides, fishing trips and a baby's first steps (not so ordinary if it's your baby), take on new meaning and become extraordinary when seen through the eyes of the person who is experiencing them.

During those years when we were creating memories through viewfinders, we didn't know we wanted a wearable camera and we couldn't imagine the difference that one would make to us. Even established camera manufacturers who had the technology at their fingertips didn't see the opportunity to change the way memories were recorded, which is probably why they just kept bringing us updated cameras with similar functionality.

In the 'needless' economy, the job of the innovator isn't to make something new; it's to make something that matters.

Story

MARKETING IS NOT A DEPARTMENT

It's 9 on Sunday night and a line of eager customers with cash in hand snakes down Victoria Street and around the corner. Not one customer who joins is surprised by the line and nobody gives up and leaves it. The effort, it seems, is clearly worth the reward.

Gelato Messina is a Sydney institution. How they make, serve and sell their product is their marketing. No full-page adverts required.

Marketing is not a department; it's the story of how you create difference for your customers.

THE PURPOSE OF BRAND STORYTELLING

When my son was growing up, there was a ritual to be upheld every September. Of course we had the usual things to do and a checklist to follow at the beginning of the school year, but what Adam really cared about more than all of that was choosing the football boots he would wear for that season. Football is more than a sport in England; it's a badge of belonging. It's also a way to bond with your peers. The boots are a part of the story the young player tells himself about what he's setting out to achieve that season and how he's going to matter.

I'm not sure how or when the Adidas Predator brand of football boots became part of Adam's story, but these were the boots he decided were 'the best', and only they would make him be 'his best'. He never, *ever* wore any other football boots. These weren't just boots, though; they were months of hopes and dreams about goals that might be scored or games that could be won with a single accurate cross, wrapped up in red leather with three silver stripes down the side.

It's easy to get caught up in the 'how to' of telling your brand story and even easier still to believe that the primary reason to invest in telling it is to sell more. But brand storytelling should primarily be the driver of participation, not sales. Storytelling is the way we enable our customers to attach meaning to our products, and it's the reason they want to belong.

When people feel like they belong—like they are part of the brand story and can own it—they become loyal customers. It turns out that the best brands in the world are a set of interdependent shared stories, a two-way experience between the customer and the brand.

The brands we really love are the ones that create difference for us. They make us feel like we belong, that we are part of their story and they are part of ours. Just like Adidas became part of my son's story when he was growing up.

THE COMPETITION ISN'T YOUR COMPETITION

Bread Society is a beautiful artisan bakery in Singapore (the website doesn't do it justice). At the back of the store, the bakers roll and knead and prove their dough in full view, whilst just in front, an assistant packages delectable breads. Self-serve cabinets filled with Chocolate Melon Brioche, Honey Lemon Danish and Sundried Tomato Bagels are lit from above by glass chandeliers. It's an experience from start to finish and a story we want to tell.

But the company doesn't want us to share it. When one of my boys tried to take a photo, he was politely informed that photography wasn't allowed. We'd missed the sign in the window.

Why go to all the trouble of telling a great story and creating a fantastic experience, only to stop the best marketing you could ever dream of from filtering out?

If you've created a brand story worth sharing, why worry about the competition? A secret sauce is worthless without people who care about what you do and why you do it. Your mission, then, isn't to prevent your idea from being copied or stolen; it's to find a way to matter.

The bigger concern for any business now is not the competition; it's obscurity.

DON'T MAKE THINGS THAT PEOPLE WANT

On a gorgeous hot summer day at the beach, you might kill for a Mr Whippy ice cream cone.

But no matter how much you want an ice cream cone today, even if that ice cream is the best you've ever tasted, you probably won't give Mr Whippy a second thought when you're back at the office tomorrow. Why is that?

When you buy ice cream from a van by the beach, you don't really want the ice cream at all. What you want is to experience the feeling of eating ice cream by the beach in that moment. After all these years, I finally understand that the tinkling music of the ice cream van that visited our neighbourhood forty years ago (before many of the homes on our street had freezers) didn't just tell us that the ice cream van was close by. It reminded us how it felt to reach up through the window in the side of the van on a long summer evening and trade two coins for five minutes of joy with a chocolate flake stuck in the top.

You might think that this is all very well if you are The Lemon Ice King of Corona in Queens, but the same rules apply to anything you can think to market. When Steve Jobs was working with his team of engineers to bring the iPhone to the world, the brief wasn't to make a touchscreen phone that could do XYZ. Jobs simply charged his team with creating the first phone people would fall in love with.

The products and services we come back to over and over again are designed for feeling, not just function. They are not made to be used or consumed. They are made to matter.

It turns out that Mr Whippy, like Steve Jobs, understood that marketing is a love story.

PRICE IS A STORY WE TELL OURSELVES

'I'm worth it.' 'It might be gone tomorrow.' 'You could make it at home for half that.' 'This is a one-off.' People pay for intangible value all the time.

Consider Uber, 'the app that connects you with a driver at the tap of a button' on your smartphone. If you simply need to get from point A to point B, why not just call or hail a taxi on the street? Well, apart from the fact that using Uber means that you don't have to wait in the rain, you don't even need to have cash or physical credit cards to pay. The real value of the service is not simply in getting people where they need to go. The value of Uber is in the perception of time saved and the elimination of uncertainty. The ability to know exactly where your driver is, and to track him with GPS as he comes to you, is something plenty of people reckon is worth paying for. People place a premium on their time. Uber doesn't need to employ the drivers or own the fleet of cars to provide value (to the tune of a rumoured $1 billion a year).

When we use a regular car hire or cab service, the sticker price may help us rationalise the decision to reach for our wallet, but when it comes to a more expensive, premium service like Uber, most of the value is created from the things we can't see (the technology that enables the driver to be there at the push of a button), and that requires us to make an emotional investment in the brand and to buy into that story.

Price and value are stories we tell ourselves. What story are your customers telling?

HOW TO TELL THE STORY OF YOUR PRODUCTS AND SERVICES

I once heard a tea taster, who tasted a thousand cups of tea a day, explain that the secret to the perfect cup of tea was the water. He said that 'water is the mother of tea'. That one phrase was enough to hold me still for a second longer. That's something we all need to learn how to do for our customers.

Let's face it: descriptions are hard. It's tough to differentiate your products and services with facts alone. Coffee is coffee, even if it is aromatic, freshly ground or single origin, right? Instead of trying to describe what it is you're selling, set out to change how people feel the moment they read your copy or visit your website.

How to create emotional points of difference with your product and service descriptions:

1. Resist relying on the description of features and benefits.
Tell people what they can do with your product, not what the product does.

2. Let your current customers do the talking.

Build trust, using proof with testimonials and customer stories.

3. Show how customers are using your product to make their lives better.

Use images, videos, case studies and stories.

4. Think about how you want the people who use your products and services to feel.

Write descriptions and create content that helps people to experience those feelings before they ever use the product or service.

5. Behave like a lover, or at least a very dear friend.

Because if you're going about your business the right way, that's exactly what you are. Now go write like one.

HOW TO TELL THE STORY OF YOUR IDEA USING THE VALUE PROPOSITION HACK

The biggest challenge that many of my clients have isn't coming up with great ideas; it's articulating why those ideas should matter, to the right people. Explaining the value of an idea can be tough if you don't have a place to start. I created the 'value proposition hack' so that you would have a way to explain the value of your idea succinctly, in just one sentence. Simply fill in the blanks and then finesse as required.

We do _____ so that you can do/feel/be _____.

We created _____ so you don't have to do/feel/be _____.

The value you create may be multi-layered, or it might be intangible (a feeling, not a physical benefit), but it still pays to write this down.

Here are some examples of value propositions which I created using the 'value proposition hack' and which could be applied to existing business ideas.

> At Method we make safe, natural cleaning products that work so that you feel good about using them. (And you don't even need to hide our beautifully designed packaging in the kitchen cupboard.)

> We created Method so that you don't have to breathe toxic fumes as you clean. (Now you can experience great cleaning results while caring for the planet, too.)

* * *

> We use only natural ingredients in Chobani so you can experience the taste of real, good, simple yogurt.

> We created Chobani so that you don't have to worry about artificial ingredients in your yogurt.

* * *

> I blog at *The Art of Non-Conformity* so that people like you, who want to change the world, can be inspired to achieve their personal goals.

> I created *The Art of Non-Conformity* so you could see that you don't have to live your life the way other people expect you to.

WHY PEOPLE PAY AND WHY IT MATTERS

The dictionary will tell you that marketing is the activity that surrounds the transfer of goods from seller to buyer. This, for that. But we also pay with time, attention and love. And even when we pay with money, it's rarely a 'this, for that' transaction, since all value is subjective.

It's easy to fall in love with your idea, but as you do, it's important to consider why someone will pay you with their time, attention, love or money, if you want that idea to create an impact in the world. In a world where the definition of value is changing, even big industries like music and publishing are having a hard time figuring this out.

First consider the reasons why your customers might pay you:

Necessity
Taxes, basic food and shelter.

Fear (in general)
Life insurance, private-school fees.

Fear of missing out
Sales, special offers, peer pressure.

Convenience
Snack size, easy open, home delivery and on and on.

Perceived value
A coke at the cinema is worth more to the popcorn eater than the coke that's at home in the fridge.

Scarcity
There is no substitute. Johnny Depp, iPod, Sydney Opera House.

Belonging

Conferences, clubs, concerts, events and online programs.

A shortcut

PayPal, Slimfast, Google.

It feels good

Kickstarter, charity donations, volunteering, books.

To reinforce the story they tell themselves and those around them.

Starbucks, Jimmy Choo shoes, French champagne, organic vegetables, gym membership, Fair Trade, Beats by Dr Dre.

It turns out that transactions are a transfer of emotion, which means that you can't tell a story to the right customers unless you understand the story they want to believe.

Which story should you be telling?

YOU DON'T HAVE TO MATTER TO EVERYONE

We weren't meant to be sitting next to each other. The European blonde, who didn't want to be separated from her boyfriend for ten hours overnight between Perth and Dubai, asked if I would mind moving to the middle seat in the row behind. So this is how I got to chatting with the chap in 36C near the end of that long flight.

He was a self-proclaimed 'left-brained engineer' and partner in a growing business.

In situations like this, I tell people I'm 'in marketing'.

I should know better.

'That's all smoke and mirrors', he said.

I smiled.

He talked a little more about the challenges that he and his partners were having in their business as they grew. I asked questions and told some stories.

Before we touched down in Dubai, he asked for my card. I warned him that it had a heart on it.

Takeaways for me and for you, too.

1. There is no excuse for being lazy about telling your story. You may not get another chance.

2. A lot of people think marketing is advertising.

3. Marketing is a transfer of emotion. We buy with our hearts and justify decisions with our heads.

4. People make judgments based on their worldview.

5. Don't try to convince people that they are wrong because you want to be right.

6. Listen twice as much as you talk.

7. Be yourself.

8. Generosity scales.

9. Always carry cards.

10. You don't have to matter to everyone.

If people don't believe you can help them, you probably can't. When they 'get it', you'll know.

WHAT STORY ARE YOU SELLING?

It feels risky to put the words 'story' and 'selling' side by side in the same sentence. 'Selling' someone on something has had a bad rap since the days of snake oil salesmen with their bogus claims, snappy taglines and half-truths designed to make people buy more of the average this or that. Although 'selling' is often seen as manipulating people into doing something they don't want to do, the truth is that it doesn't matter who you are or what you do; as soon as you get out of the shower every morning, you're selling a story.

All markets, industries, tribes, leaders and individuals sell stories. We have to. We don't have a choice, because stories are how humans read each other.

My husband has been a doctor for more than twenty-five years. He was a medical student when we met. We've had many a long walk punctuated by a conversation about what makes people tick. He's told me stories of examining babies and the way they look deep into your eyes, searching, as you press the cool metal of the stethoscope on their chest. They're already looking to make sense of the story. And as we grow up, each time we see a doctor, we strengthen the association between the stethoscope and the person who has earned the right to wear one. Studies have shown that we are more likely to trust a man wearing a stethoscope than one who doesn't. Doctors sell trust by getting the grades to go to medical school in the first place, by doing the time and then behaving in a way that reinforces our worldview.

Medicine doesn't sell cures, it sells trust. The lottery sells hope (it might be you), and many brands sell a promise of a better version of ourselves. Tiffany sells mattering, BootsnAll sells non-conformist adventure, Facebook sells belonging and Wholefoods sells nurturing and self-love.

You are not selling coffee, concert tickets, books, lipstick, yogurt, entertainment or information.

You're selling a story. It's never been more important to know which one.

WAS EVERYTHING OKAY?

The table was clean. The waitress arrived to take coffee orders within a couple of minutes. We tried to ignore the peeling corners of the laminated menu.

The food and the coffee were fine. The waitress was polite in a 'going through the motions' kind of way. Her parting question as we paid the bill: 'Was everything okay?'

Yes, actually, everything *was* okay. We had no complaints, nothing to report, and that, I guess, is the problem for most businesses—and it's also the opportunity for you. Every day we have experiences that are nothing to write home about, micro make-or-break moments. Feelings that exist but that we can't explain. Changing how we feel in those moments is so important that Apple has a secret packaging room where designers test which box designs evoke an emotional response.

My friend Stuart Hall, who is an entrepreneur and gifted app developer, once told me that what differentiates a great app from a good one is the feeling that a level of love has been put into it. Living in a digital age has conditioned us to expect that things happen on demand and work perfectly the first time and every time. The goal posts for exceptional have shifted, and it's almost impossible to make a product or service fly now without that level of love.

We simply know it when we feel it. We don't want everything to be okay anymore.

We want to feel the love.

SUCCESS IS HOW YOUR CUSTOMERS FEEL

You've just had a great launch. You made your monthly sales targets. Your stock sold out in one day. There are a hundred and one reasons to celebrate, and there is one thing to remember.

Success is not just a data point that you hit on the sales chart, or a dollar figure that makes your accountant happy. Success is how your customers feel.

How are you measuring that?

WHAT IF YOU HAD ONE LINE TO TELL THE TRUTH ABOUT YOUR PRODUCT?

Imagine that you have a giant billboard on which to tell your customers the truth about your product or service. You've got just one line to do it in.

What would your truth look and sound like? Is the truth in that single sentence what you want it to be?

If not, what do you need to do in order to rewrite it?

(It probably doesn't involve buying a billboard.)

WE NEED TO STOP TELLING OUR CUSTOMERS WHAT WE DO

I'm driving along behind the white Ezy Tiles van when we stop at a red light and I get close enough to read their sales pitch, which is an image and a single line.

The picture shows three guys wearing dust masks that look like something you'd see in a documentary about chemical warfare. Each man is brandishing some kind of heavy-duty drill that looks like it could demolish a room in minutes. The dust cloud that surrounds them obliterates the view of the river from the balcony in the background.

'We remove tiles and floors', the tagline on the white van shouts at me.

'No, you don't', I can't help thinking. 'You come into my home and leave a trail of dust and destruction in your wake.'

While I might need old tiles to be removed, what I really want is a smooth, level surface to lay my gorgeous new tiles on.

It (almost) goes without saying that your process needs to delight customers every step of the way. But your customers don't want to know what you do. They want to know how you're going to enable them to do what they want to do.

There's a reason IKEA leaves the instructions and the confusing assortment of screws inside the packaging. Nobody wants to buy the tortuous process of assembling that piece of furniture; we just want some shelves for our books or a table for our dinner.

People almost never buy the process. They buy the result. We really should be selling them what they want to be sold.

STOP SELLING STUFF, START SELLING STORIES

David is a genius who happens to sell for a living. I watched him sell a $150 pair of UGG boots to a woman who had been killing time by wandering through his souvenir shop with no big agenda one wet Friday afternoon.

He began not by asking what she was looking for, as many salespeople would, but by asking *who* she was looking for. From there, questions and answers easily flowed. The age of the woman's granddaughter. The story about how she was always asking her grandma to buy her a pair of 'expensive fake UGG boots back home'. The grandma's concerns about how they might damage her granddaughter's feet or make them smell.

David handled each of her responses effortlessly, like arranging pieces of a jigsaw puzzle into a solution. He dispelled the woman's fears, one by one, and gained her trust. Then, and only then, did he reflect back to her the story of the moment when Grandma would hand the boots over to her granddaughter, in the special reusable bag that would be 'shown off to friends at school'.

'I might even get a hug for these', she said, as she handed over three fifty-dollar notes.

And there, expressed in that single sentence, was what David had already known.

The best salespeople, marketers and brands don't actually sell us stuff they've made in factories or built with lines of code. They don't even sell us things we want or need. They simply sell us the story that we already want to live and believe.

WHO IS YOUR CUSTOMER?

Joan works as a personal trainer at the local gym. She looks old enough to be someone's grandma, but I don't think she is. Unlike most women her age who live around here, Joan doesn't wear a wedding ring. She visits the same café for breakfast every day, but not at the same time because some days she has a client at 5.30am. On those days she goes straight to the café afterwards. She always eats alone, drinks a skinny latte and normally has toast. When she decides to 'mix it up a bit', she tells the staff she's in the mood for a change today. She seems to struggle with her weight and wrestles with herself over whether to spread butter on her toast—some days she doesn't.

All of the staff at the café know her by name, and they don't seem to mind when she reminds them that they have forgotten to turn the music down or the lights on. Joan doesn't sit at the same table every day like some of the other regular customers. That tiny decision is her way of telling herself that she's not stuck in a rut. We can tell that she lives close by because this neighbourhood café is not the kind of place people visit every day unless they have a reason to come, and it's not the kind of place people drive across town to experience. But then Joan is not really here for coffee and toast.

If I were the café owner, I'd be working harder to make Joan feel like I cared that she showed up every day. I'd want to show her that she mattered.

Tell me about your customer. Not just her age, income and postcode— tell me who she really is.

What keeps her awake at night? Where does she spend her time, both online and offline? What does she care about? Tell me about her fears, hopes and dreams. What matters to her?

Tell me everything you know. Find out what you don't.

If we don't take the time to really see our customers and get to know their story, how can we create the things and experiences they want and need? They are giving us clues every day; we just need to open our eyes and, more importantly, our hearts.

BECOME PART OF THE STORY

I arranged to meet one of my Twitter friends for the first time in the little bar at the front of my hotel. He is a designer from London, and as luck would have it, we were visiting New York at the same time (something we discovered through our simultaneous posts of Times Square on Instagram).

We met, we drank, we chatted. 'I'm surprised you're staying in a hotel', he said. 'My partner and I have scored a really cool place on Airbnb. It's got a giant blackboard in the kitchen and it's big enough to play Frisbee indoors.'

How I chose to travel didn't fit with the story Tom had constructed about me. The kind of people who meet on Twitter, whose work gives them freedom to travel—people with blogs, who discover that their friends are in New York by checking Instagram—don't stay in hotels. And very, very soon, they will not be queueing for a black taxi in London or hailing a yellow cab from the sidewalk in New York, because riding with Uber will be one of the ways they signal that they belong.

We are the stories we tell ourselves. The choices we make—from whom we follow on Twitter, to how we experience a city, where we shop and what we buy—have become as big a part of our identity as the place where we were born.

Buying is no longer about getting things we need. It's about reinforcing a set of beliefs we hold and share. Marketing is not about finding new ways to sell more of something. It's about affinity more than it's about price—feelings more than facts. Marketing is about giving people frames of reference and context. And above all, marketing is about becoming part of peoples' stories.

Where I Hope We're Headed

SHIFTING THE FOCUS FROM RESULTS TO RELATIONSHIPS

More than thirty years on from those days when clipboards, pencils and manpower were replaced by barcodes, algorithms and analytics, it's easy to believe that technological leaps have made us more successful in delivering what people want. The truth is that massive shifts in what's technologically possible haven't made a blind bit of difference to the biology of humans. The needs and wants of people haven't changed all that much—we are still driven by instinct and emotions and our basic human need to belong. And the way we typically do business still doesn't take the fundamentals of basic human nature into account often enough.

There's still a problem with how performance is measured both by us and in our organisations. Typically you have a budget and targets to achieve. The purpose of the budget is to make sales go up or waiting times go down. Our systems are designed to judge and reward us on results. If the campaign you authorised sold more beans and fish fingers last quarter, then that's a win. But if the only way you can get sales to go up is to spend money on a campaign to make sales go up, then you're going to have to keep spending money on campaigns to make sales go up.

I've seen brand managers ride the wave of fantastic public awareness campaigns that boosted their results in the short term, only to see sales come crashing back down a couple of months later as the awareness they had engineered evaporated along with their advertising budget. And so the cycle perpetuates. They spend more to get more. While it might keep some businesses and ad agencies afloat for a little while, this is not a sustainable strategy. There is no shortcut to mattering to your customers.

It's a lot harder to justify building little by little for the long term, because we are constantly measuring and measured by short-term results. If you apply for a promotion or a new role, your employer wants to see the sales figures; she needs metrics as proof that you've done your job. And so we work hardest of all to give others (and ourselves) something to measure. We look for quick wins and easy targets, which reinforce the notion that we're doing our job. Sometimes we just end up measuring the wrong things, and in doing so, we subconsciously demonstrate to the people we should be serving that we're not in it for the long haul.

When Warby Parker released its first fun and quirky annual report, it led to their three biggest sales days at the time. Something that was designed to delight customers became an accidental marketing tool.

> 'It very much fit into our philosophy of being
> transparent. We find [that] the more information we
> share, the more vulnerable we are, and that [includes]
> sharing the positive and the warts—the deeper
> relationship we build with our customers.'
> —NEIL BLUMENTHAL, CO-FOUNDER, WARBY PARKER

Companies like Warby Parker are lighting the way and blazing a trail for a new breed of entrepreneur to follow. They are not only showing us that it's possible to profit by building a values-based business; they are also proving that finding ways to delight and get closer to our customers is actually the shortcut to success.

What if we optimised our businesses, our organisations and our cultures for relationships first and results second? What if we focused less on creating awareness and more on generating trust? What if we traded quick wins for loyalty? What if we looked up from our clipboards or analytics and connected with our customers? What if we stopped trying to be seen and learned how to see instead?

What might the real gains be then?

Acknowledgements

Thank you for buying this book, for supporting these ideas and for daring to believe that what you put out into the world and call 'work' might have something to do with love.

Thanks to Seth Godin for helping me to take the first step on this journey. I want to thank Reese Spykerman for designing another amazing cover, our fourth one together. It's not easy to tell the story of an idea in a single visual and no one does it better than her. Thanks to Catherine Oliver for being the best editor a girl could wish for and to Kelly Exeter for being the most patient designer on the planet, for her hard work on the interior of the paperback.

Thanks to my blog readers for coming back and making it easy for me to keep showing up to write about the things that I see. Without you, I would have no reason to write or to do the work that I love.

If you are a new reader, you can get regular free updates about marketing and brand storytelling from my blog, at www.thestoryoftelling.com.

I look forward to sharing more ideas with you there.

References

INTRODUCTION

'You've got to find what you love' — '"You've got to find what you love", Jobs says.' *Stanford University News.* 14 June 2005. <http://news. stanford.edu/news/2005/june15/jobs-061505.html>.

WHAT'S LOVE GOT TO DO WITH IT?

Research conducted into how people are persuaded — (1) Robert Cialdini and Steve Martin, 'Secrets from the Science of Persuasion' <https://www.youtube.com/watch?v=cFdCzN7RYbw>. (2) Dennis T. Regan, 'Effects of a favor and liking on compliance'. *Journal of Experimental Social Psychology*, vol. 7, issue 6 (November 1971): 627–639. (3) Robert B. Cialdini, *Influence: Science and Practice.* Allyn and Bacon, 2001.

We give bigger tips — David B. Strohmetz, Bruce Rind, Reed Fisher and Michael Lynn, 'Sweetening the Till: The Use of Candy to Increase Restaurant Tipping'. *Journal of Applied Social Psychology,* vol. 32, issue 2 (February 2002): 300–309. <http://tippingresearch.com/uploads/ Candy_Manuscript.pdf>.

STRATEGY

HOW TO WRITE A MISSION STATEMENT—AND TWENTY GREAT MISSION STATEMENTS TO INSPIRE YOU

By definition a mission statement — 'Mission statement'. Dictionary.com. <http://dictionary.reference.com/browse/mission+statement?s=t>.

Academic papers have been written — See, for example, Christopher K. Bart, 'Sex, Lies, and Mission Statements'. Business Horizons (Nov–Dec. 1997): 9–18.

The handy mission statement generator — <http://cmorse.org/missiongen/>.

Various mission statement examples — From the corresponding companies' or individuals' websites.

WHY WE ADVERTISE

Ad spending is set to increase — Suzanne Vranica, 'Ad Outlays Expected To Pick Up Pace in '14'. *The Wall Street Journal*, 9 December 2013. <http://online.wsj.com/news/articles/SB20001424052702303330204579246003193822532>

WHAT CUSTOMERS BELIEVE IS YOUR COMPETITIVE ADVANTAGE

Today that number is just 28% — Horace Dediu, 'The Five Year Plan'. Asymco, 10 October 2013. <http://www.asymco.com/2013/10/10/the-five-year-plan/>.

HOW TO GET THE WORLD TO BEAT A PATH TO YOUR DOOR

'Make others successful' — Goke Pelemo, 'The Culture Code, from IDEO'. Goke's Musings. <https://goke.me/the-culture-code-from-ideo/>

GREAT CONTENT MARKETING DOESN'T FEEL LIKE MARKETING

'You're more likely to summit Mount Everest ....' – 'Jonathan Perelman: Content Is King, But Distribution Is Queen'. 99U. <http://99u.com/videos/23015/jonathan-perelman-content-is-king-distribution-is-queen>

The return on investment from advertising — Kevin J. Clancy and Randy L. Stone, 'Don't Blame the Metrics'. *Harvard Business Review*, June 2005. <http://hbr.org/2005/06/dont-blame-the-metrics/ar/1>

THINKING ABOUT MARKETING AS A STRATEGY FOR GROWTH, NOT JUST SALES

The modern marketers at technology startups — 'Growth Hacking'. *Wikipedia.* <http://en.wikipedia.org/wiki/Growth_hacking>

Hotels in New York lost out — Jeremy Rifkin, 'The Rise of the Sharing Economy'. *Los Angeles Times,* 6 April 2014. <http://www.latimes.com/opinion/op-ed/la-oe-rifkin-airbnb-20140406-story.html#axzz2yBuRs0hz>

HOW TO HIT YOUR TARGET

The point of aim is always closer — 'How to Aim'. *The Archery Library.* <http://www.archerylibrary.com/books/stemmler/essentials-of-archery/docs/how-to-aim.html>

WHAT'S MORE IMPORTANT THAN BUILDING AWARENESS?

In a world where it's harder to get attention — Wenlei Ma, 'No One's Paying Attention to Digital Ads... Well, 8% Are'. *AdNews*, 13 June 2013. <http://www.adnews.com.au/adnews/no-one-s-paying-attention-to-digital-ads-well-8-are>

ATTENTION IS A TWO-WAY STREET

Zappos built a billion-dollar business — Natalie Sisson, 'Delivering Happiness—A Billion Dollar Business Lesson From Zappos'. *Forbes*, 2 September 2010. <http://www.forbes.com/sites/work-in-progress/2010/09/02/delivering-happiness-a-billion-dollar-business-lesson-from-zappos/>

PICK ONE THING

Apple chooses to lead with design — 'Designed by Apple in California'. Apple Inc. <http://www.apple.com/designed-by-apple/>

THE BUSINESS CASE FOR CREATING GREAT CUSTOMER EXPERIENCES

According to a report — 'The Cost of Poor Customer Service: The Economic Impact of the Customer Experience and Engagement in 16 Key Economies'. Genesys Telecommunication Laboratories. <http://www.marketingdeservicios.com/wp-content/uploads/Genesys_Global_Survey09_screen.pdf>

CONTEXT

HOW APPLE SUCCEEDED WHILE OTHERS FAILED

When Apple designed their first store — 'Steve Jobs Introduces the Apple Store (2001)'. Posted on YouTube by vintagemacmuseum. <https://www.youtube.com/watch?v=xLTNfIaL5YI&feature=share&list=PL420EB3CF59FD5354&index=1>

THE BIGGEST PROBLEM FACING ENTREPRENEURS

What made the Segway falter — Mike Masnick, 'Why Segway Failed To Reshape the World: Focused On Invention, Rather Than Innovation'. *Techdirt*, 31 July 2009. <https://www.techdirt.com/articles/20090730/1958335722.shtml>

What made Blackberry fall into the abyss — Zach Epstein, 'BlackBerry Usage Share Plummets to Just 1% in the U.S.' BGR, 16 August 2012. <http://bgr.com/2012/08/16/blackberry-market-share-us-2012-usage/>

What made Kodak flounder — Beth Jinks, 'Kodak Moments Just a Memory as Company Exits Bankruptcy'. *Bloomberg*, 3 September 2013. <http://www.bloomberg.com/news/2013-09-03/kodak-exits-bankruptcy-as-printer-without-photographs.html>

THE TROUBLE WITH POSITIONING

President Obama negotiated to keep his BlackBerry — Andy Sullivan, 'Obama Keeps BlackBerry, After All'. *Reuters*, 22 January 2009. <http://www.reuters.com/article/2009/01/22/us-obama-blackberry-idUSTRE50L6H820090122>

Four years ago, RIM was the fastest-growing company — '100 Fastest-Growing Companies'. *Fortune*, 31 August 2009. <http://archive.fortune.com/magazines/fortune/fortunefastestgrowing/2009/snapshots/1.html>

A market share of 47% — Ian Austen and Jennifer Daniel, 'When BlackBerry Reigned (the Queen Got One!), and How It Fell'. *The New York Times*, 28 September 2013. <http://www.nytimes.com/interactive/2013/09/29/technology/when-blackberry-reigned-the-queen-got-one-and-how-it-fell.html?ref=business&_r=0>

THE MOST DANGEROUS THING ABOUT YOUR COMPETITION

While taxi firms worried — Danny Gold, 'Taxi Fare Increase in Effect'. *The Wall Street Journal*, 4 September 2012. <http://online.wsj.com/news/articles/SB10000872396390044384740457763188171595 6216>

Built a company with an $18 billion valuation — Evelyn M. Rusli and Douglas MacMillan, 'Uber Gets an Uber-Valuation'. *The Wall Street Journal*, 6 June 2014. <http://online.wsj.com/articles/uber-gets-uber-valuation-of-18-2-billion-1402073876>

HOW TO SELL A GUITAR

Can't effectively communicate the value — 'The Most Effective Sales Strategy Is a Great Message'. Corporate Visions. <http://corporatevisions.com/resources/article-archive/the-most-effective-sales-strategy-is-a-great-message/>

EMPATHY IS THE KILLER APP

Google Glass and the lack of empathy — Robert Scoble, Facebook post. <https://www.facebook.com/RobertScoble/posts/10152350351549655?stream_ref=18>

Teaching Glass users how to be empathetic — (1) 'Google Glass: Don't Be a Glasshole'. *Mashable.* <https://www.youtube.com/watch?v=FlfZ9FNC99k> (2) Matt Burns, 'Google Explains How Not To Be A Glasshole'. *TechCrunch*, 18 February 2014. <http://techcrunch.com/2014/02/18/google-explains-how-not-to-be-a-glasshole/>

WHO DECIDES WHAT WINS

Customers pushed back — Arthur Martin, 'Revolt Over Cadbury's "Rounder, Sweeter" Bars'. *Mail Online*, 15 September 2013. <http://www.dailymail.co.uk/news/article-2421568/Revolt-Cadburys-rounder-sweeter-bars-Not-classic-rectangle-shape-Dairy-Milk-changed-customers-also-sugary.html>

THE VALUE OF ASKING 'WHAT IF?'

Housekeeping can feel like more of an intrusion — Lucky, 'Hotels: Show Us Some Innovation When It Comes to Privacy/Housekeeping!' *One Mile at a Time*, 8 July 2011. <http://onemileatatime.boardingarea.com/2011/07/08/hotels-show-us-some-innovation-when-it-comes-to-privacyhousekeeping/>

It costs a hotel $22 a day — Beth Cone, 'Average Hotel Housekeeping Costs'. *eHow.* <http://www.ehow.com/facts_5974168_average-hotel-housekeeping-costs.html>

THE ECONOMICS OF ATTENTION

Translated into less trust — Sarah Vizard, 'Majority of UK Consumers Don't Trust Brands' Advertising'. *Marketing Week*, 9 April 2014. <http://www.marketingweek.co.uk/sectors/technology-and-telecoms/news/majority-of-uk-consumers-dont-trust-brands-advertising/4010029.article>

The cost of paid attention has been rising — Thales S. Teixeira, 'The Rising Cost of Consumer Attention: Why You Should Care, and What You Can Do about It'. *Harvard Business Review* working paper, 17 January 2014. <http://www.hbs.edu/faculty/Publication%20Files/14-055_2ef21e7e-7529-4864-b0f0-c64e4169e17f.pdf>

HOW TO BE GREAT

'The right song at the right time …' — Ian C. Rogers, 'Beats Music Is Here'. *Beats Music Blog.* <http://blog.beatsmusic.com/beats-music-is-here/>

WHAT ARE YOUR CUSTOMERS' TRIGGERS?

A simple formula for behaviour change — Dr BJ Fogg, 'BJ Fogg's Behavior Model'. <http://www.behaviormodel.org/>

THE PURPOSE OF INNOVATION IN A 'NEEDLESS' ECONOMY

Where more people have mobile phones — Yue Wang, 'More People Have Cell Phones Than Toilets, U.N. Study Shows'. *Time.com*, 25 March 2013. <http://newsfeed.time.com/2013/03/25/more-people-have-cell-phones-than-toilets-u-n-study-shows/>

Changes what they come to expect — Emily Wax, 'In India, More Women Demand Toilets Before Marriage'. *The Washington Post*, 12 October 2009. <http://www.washingtonpost.com/wp-dyn/content/article/2009/10/11/AR2009101101934.html>

STORY

DON'T MAKE THINGS THAT PEOPLE WANT

The first phone people would fall in love with — Andrew Wray, 'Former Apple Manager Tells How the Original iPhone Was Developed, Why It Went With Gorilla Glass'. *iMore*, 4 February 2012. <http://www.imore.com/apple-manager-tells-original-iphone-born>

PRICE IS A STORY WE TELL OURSELVES

Uber, to the tune of a rumoured $1 billion a year — Matthew Panzarino, 'Leaked Uber Numbers, Which We've Confirmed, Point To Over $1B Gross, $213M Revenue.' *TechCrunch*, 4 December 2013. <http://techcrunch.com/2013/12/04/leaked-uber-numbers-which-weve-confirmed-point-to-over-1b-gross-revenue-213m-revenue/>

WHAT STORY ARE YOU SELLING?

We are more likely to trust a man wearing a stethoscope — Moyez Jiwa, et al. 'Impact of the Presence of Medical Equipment in Images on Viewers' Perceptions of the Trustworthiness of an Individual On-Screen'. *Journal of Medical Internet Research*, 14.4 (2012): e100. *MEDLINE*.

WAS EVERYTHING OKAY?

Apple has a secret packaging room — Neil Hughes, 'Book Details Apple's "Packaging Room", Steve Jobs's Interest in Advanced Cameras'. *Apple Insider,* 24 January 2012. <http://appleinsider.com/articles/12/01/24/book_details_apples_packaging_room_interests_in_advanced_cameras_>

WHERE I HOPE WE'RE HEADED

'It very much fit into our philosophy' — Ann-Christine Diaz, 'Warby Parker Unveils 2013 Annual Report—and It's 365 Days Long'. *Advertising Age,* 10 January 2014. <http://adage.com/article/news/warby-parker-unveils-365-day-2013-annual-report/291006/>

CPSIA information can be obtained
at www.ICGtesting.com
Printed in the USA
BVOW06s2041261216
471866BV00001B/103/P